Uncertain Verse

Vinod Anand

BookLeaf Publishing

India | USA | UK

Made with ♥ on the BookLeaf Publishing Platform
www.bookleafpub.in
www.bookleafpub.com

Dedication

Above all
for
Giri, Shefali, Akshay, Ayushi,
Sheeba, Nemo, Inji, Mani.

for the
Rishi Valley Class of '81

Without you, I am not.

Acknowledgement

Thanks to all my English teachers, who will be tearing out their hair, if they ever read this.

'Punctuations? For heaven's sake'!

Sorry. Thought has no commas, colons or full stops.

Thanks to my family for understanding me because I speak like I write... or is it the other way around? Thanks to all my schoolmates... you are my extended family.

Thank you JK, you encouraged me to question.

Preface

Are these poems? Is this Poetry? If the penning of thought directly onto paper is a criterion, perhaps this is. But, if thought needs to pass through the filter of rhythm and rhyme, perhaps, this isn't.

This is an unfiltered, unedited transcription of random musings and feelings.

Some rhyme.
Some won't.
Some hurt.
Some don't.

Punctuation has been left out, in most places. I wanted the reader to find their own rhythm, meter, beat... whatever.

These aren't just my thoughts...
perhaps...
they're yours too.

Musings on a Monday

and there i sat...

looking out at a foggy past...

and a not-so-clear future...

the present was lost

between memories and expectations...

will the future be a dream...

or a watercolour portrait of the past...

will the tears from a life, tainted...

wash it all away

and paint the hues of a future...

in acrylics and oils...

pastels and hope...

will tomorrow herald the future...

or will it be today's fantasy...

teardrops and rain...

expectations and pain...

bring out the umbrellas...

it's monsoon time

and nothing to gain...

You Lied

i saw the light,

but it was a flame.

i smelt you,

my mother

you weren't the same.

i was born in the water,

of her womb,

not yours.

now my tears,

it seems,

will drown me again.

i see the moon above me,

it's a noose.

i lived. i felt.

i hurt. i cried.

i laughed.

i smiled.

i fooled myself.

for a while.

But,

you lied.

you lied.

you lied.

I died.

A Life

in gentle morning light

in my mother's lap

covered in dew

i am born.

spreading my fragrance

tiny heart beating

with joy and anxiety

at seeing a world

so beautiful and vast.

dropped in a basket

cruelly picked away

i didn't complain

i smiled as i lay

before random Gods.

but my beauty withers

my fragrance fades

replaced by incense

i am sick.

no water no food

no morning light.

i wither

i fade

i breathe my last

i have become an outcast.

even as i lie

in a dustbin to die

i manage to smile

a last hurrah

a defiant try.

a few days from now

at my mother's feet

i'll lie

to nurture her young

for them to die.

how callous you were

you offered me

to your Gods

never thought of me

as a mortal.

complain, i did not.

my job is done

my beauty gone

my fragrance too

but even in death

i do for my family

all i can do.

do you?

I am just a flower

to you.

goodbye.

adieu.

Same Difference

in my dreams i awake

in a world unworldly.

my love is my hate

and reality my fate.

i'm hardly soft

i'm silently loud.

i'm sadly happy

and ashamedly proud.

i'm nakedly dressed

i'm calmly distressed.

i'm young but i'm old

and i'm shyly bold.

i'm good yet bad

i'm sanely mad.

i'm a manly feminine

a canine feline.

i'm an introverted extrovert

a conservative pervert.

i subvert to divert

and continue to revert.

i surely confuse

i accept to refuse.

i silently shout

i was in, i want out.

transwoman transman

in woman there's man.

take a stand sitting down

he/she is my pronoun.

wake up in your sleep

and blindly see.

i'm locked up no more

I am, finally, free.

Rain on me

clouds, they gather

from crimson born

billowing and huffing

obliterating the morn

stealing the sky

that once was blue

all that remains

is grey in many hues

the sky growls

a desperate protest

eyes flash anger

thoughts put to rest

then it breaks down

acid drops of rain

nobody to share

these decades of pain

the people they scamper

scurrying for cover

support group they said

but they just let you suffer

the muck it flows

dirt in the drains

'tis not blood anymore

that flows in my veins

the sun, it did try

to break through the gloom

a brave, losing battle

a foreteller of doom

there's no fight left

no purpose, no aim

there'll be no rainbows

just regrets remain

i've fought the battles

and the scars don't heal

see me, oh father

before you i kneel

slash, cut deep

let it flow out

watch the crimson flow

let there be no doubt

the clouds they gather

they're of crimson born

only darkness remains

there's no sign of morn.

Friend

the awkwardness

at the first meeting

the stuttered name

initials, surname and all

sitting adjacent

backbenchers bond

standing in the corner

giggling

secrets stored

in bush shirt pockets

my friend.

He...

test paper boats

on a muddy stream

puddles and potholes

mud-covered BATA Jawans

quick pull on a

rain-laden branch

screeches and curses

six drenched girls

redtail lizards

in a Camlin box

snakes in the dorm

He took...

love notes to 'that' gal

pressed flowers in texts

midnight panty raids

exciting tuck-shop days

furtive meets after curfew

cement beds

checked counterpanes

tender tamarinds

roasted on a fire

special eggs for breakfast

a fruit salad barter

He took it...

a Debonair centrefold

under silk cotton mattresses

Nick Carter and Herman Hesse

scorpions and dragonflies

strings on their tail

stomping on snails

tadpoles in Horlicks bottles

cheat slips in shoes

all this

and more

the bastard

He took it all.

Libellulidae

I soar. I hover. I fly away.

Anisoptera. Libellulidae.

Rainbows on my wings

Kaleidoscopic eyes

Flitting between sunbeams

Before sparrows arise.

I soar. I hover. I fly away.

Anisoptera. Libellulidae.

Resting on petals

splashed with colours divine

Sipping on dewdrops

on the whisker of a dandelion

I soar. I hover. I fly away.

Anisoptera. Libellulidae.

Breakfast on a poesy

Lunch on a rose

snacks on a daisy

End of day is close

I soar. I hover. I fly away.

Anisoptera. Libellulidae.

Soaring on thermals

like a fancy drone

With my friends and my family

I am never alone

I soar. I hover. I fly away.

Anisoptera. Libellulidae.

You've got to be careful

of those mischievous boys

Tie a string to your tail

they'll use you as toys

I soar. I hover. I fly away.

Anisoptera. Libellulidae.

Duck away from cars

their headlights are bright

Make one mistake

You'll never see the light

I soar. I hover. I fly away.

Anisoptera. Libellulidae.

Three days to fly

that's all we've got

Wonder why He did that

that funny fellow, God

I soar. I hover. I fly away.

Anisoptera. Libellulidae.

I'm not complaining

I've just got no time

As long as I'm here

this world is all mine

I soar. I hover. I fly away.

Anisoptera. Libellulidae.

You'll find me fallen

frozen in death

Rainbows on my wings

Kaleidoscope. No breath.

I soar. I hover. I fly away.

Anisoptera. Libellulidae.

First Day. First Show.

Tinsel dreams

shimmering between

paddy field bunds.

Coconut palms

with celluloid smiles

cows with violin bells

goats singing

choral farewells.

You've got it

they said.

You are a star.

Go to the city,

take the plunge.

First Day.

First Show.

Keep tickets for us.

The music changed

no shimmering lights

You're dark.

No class. No style.

and armpit hair! oh my!

Your Tamil's good.

average atleast.

Heroine's friend

the girl in one scene.

Try new-age directors

possibly get a break

they sniggered.

Get a portfolio

these pictures

they're crap.

Bend down

turn around.

Look left

look right.

You've got nice tits

It's a 'look' test.

show it!

1000 watt fireflies

flashing around.

Paraffin eyes

devouring

deriding

disrobing

describing.

Adjust!

you've got to.

Wanna be a star

don't you?

What're you hiding

behind 6 yards of shame?

Show me more flesh

Spread 'em again.

It started with one

but the others came soon

one after another

standing in queue.

A casting couch game

No rules.

No dice.

Producer.

Financier.

Director.

Manager.

Star.

Him too.

Lights! Camera!

Action.

Threats hidden

in kilobyte reels.

The paddy fields withered.

No rain, No water.

The cows were slaughtered

goats quartered.

No role.

No shoot.

No star.

Just numbers.

2

customers tonight.

1000

for 1 shot?

69

you bitch!

Think you're some star?

Coconut fibers

they smell of her village.

Each one

carries a tale

A screenplay.

A true story.

A tragedy.

A brown ceiling fan

a Nilkamal stool.

The smell of dark cowsheds

urine soaked.

The train

in the distance

wails.

The title song

of her first film.

First Day.

First Show.

Tickets for all.

Patchouli and Rot

oft' times

i wander

through the catacombs

of my mind

'tis not easy

'tis painful

scary

cobweb memories

hang

dusty grey wisps

embracing time

black doors

brass locks

ageing

greenish blue

rusty hinges

scream

unwilling to part

let the uneasy

equilibrium

last

compromises

like stinking rats

scurry

spindly footprints

disturb

dubious decisions

left painfully interred

fungus and water stains

a giant Rorschach

safeguarding secrets

bipolar thoughts

empty echoes

bouncing of walls

receding into darkness

no trace

no recall

empty liquor bottles

of emotions repressed

the spirit has left

the smell

tantalisingly fresh

with festering wounds

arms reach out

to deceive

to snuff out

no chains here

no fetters

yesterday's dust

is a 16 lever

padlock

an earthen lamp

hides frightened

in a corner

no oil, no wick

no flame

lips blackened

by blurted words

spilled haemoglobin

betel juice stains

wrap around me

embrace me

musty brown blanket

of time

i wait

for your

muddy earthen notes

patchouli and rot

I'm comfortable now

no more

wandering about.

Autopsy

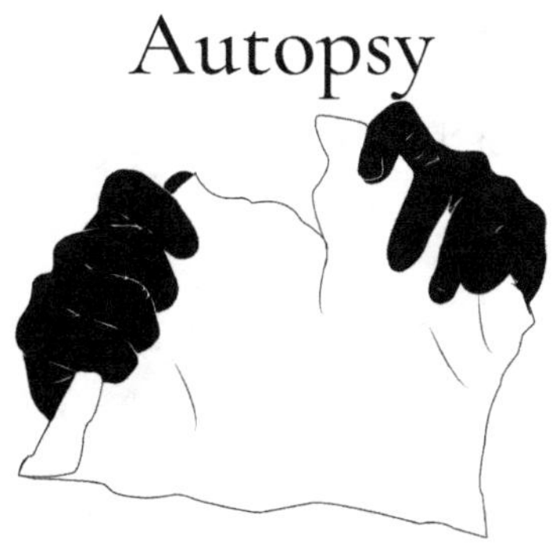

you walked

anonymous.

another 'white coat'

another intern.

he didn't see you

he saw lust

he saw power.

he didn't hear the scream

he smothered it.

like your dream.

your moan

a lament

for so much left undone

the painful gasp

a story oft' told

of capitation fees

pawned heirlooms

and mortgaged homes.

he couldn't see

in your eyes

the light going out.

he couldn't see

the battles you fought.

his every thrust

his every touch

hot iron rods.

branding.

marking.

labelling you, woman.

an object of desire.

he tasted your sweat

of years of toil.

he caressed the scars

the blisters, the boils.

he inhaled with glee

the perfume

of your death.

he touched

in doubt

like Thomas did

not checking for life

but the absence of it.

and now they scramble.

squabble and babble.

ideology and rights.

politics and strife.

dissecting your life

with timelines

drawn from lazy clocks.

they measure

his guilt

in milligrams of sperm

ejaculated perversion

bondage and porn.

not even a name

do you carry in death.

a 'medical intern'

you remain, at best.

on a steel bed

you lie.

dissected.

your wounds

mere exhibits

for legalese debated.

and you lie.

alone

abandoned

afraid

again.

but outside

they clamour

with callous disdain.

flashbulbs

bright lights.

you're a headline now

to gain from

to remonstrate,

bring out your banners

it's time to demonstrate.

you're nirbhaya 2

or is it 62?

you're just a statistic

'she got raped too'.

i stand in the crowd

like many others do

just another father.

but, i know.

i know, with you,

i've lost another daughter.

Sphygmomanometer

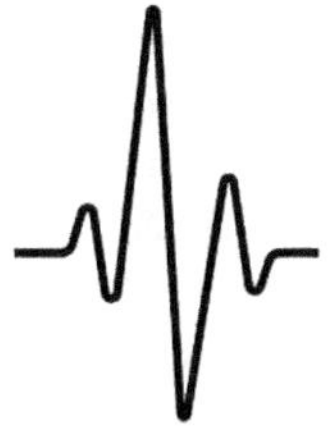

have you stood and watched

a breath escape

from lips pursed

unwilling to let go?

have you seen a breast

withered by age

fight the last beat,

let go?

have you looked

with trepidation

at a sphygmomanometer

and wondered,

isn't there a simpler word,

for that which is taking

my granny away?

as the paddles buzz with charge,

i question existence

have you wondered why

every dawn brings yearning?

why every day is a beginning?

why eternity is a dream,

destroyed by dawn?

i hate tomorrows.

they spell hope

unfulfilled, unfound.

i live in my yesterdays

idiotic expectations

fairytale fantasies.

i wait for closures

where there are none.

i wait.

for the breath to escape.

to carry my tomorrows

to a space far away.

my breath is held tight.

my eyes transfixed.

on the pursed lips.

the broken ribs.

i want her to fight.

Beat the stupid machine.

whack down that mercury column.

do it for me

i'm broken i'm beaten.

i wait. i wait for

a gasp, a sign.

the paddles buzz

her body jacks up.

the mercury slides down.

the sphygmomanometer won.

Happy Pandora

write about happiness

they said

i smiled. i tried.

the words wouldn't flow

the ink dried up

the pencil became a leaden stub

but, i dug

deep into the past

buried somewhere

was a wooden chest

locked. forgotten.

here, happiness lay at rest

little stolen moments

tiny sparks of joy

innocent proposals

hesitant confessions

locked away they lie

they never seem to die

cotton candy cheeks

sticky finger trails

bright green lollipop

picked off the ground

apply the 10-second rule

they never taught at school

a couple working hard

atop a merry-go-round

tiny, wooden giant wheels

propelled off the ground

trails of sparks over beach sand

spicy, roasted corn in hand

taffy watches

teeming with flies

a roadside ice cream, milk stick

what a loud, slurpy, drippy lick

ice shavings in a mud cup

gaudy coloured liquid, drunk up

wrinkled old granny

selling gram and gooseberries

single side, ruled notebooks

pilot pens, Bata shoes

Royal Blue, Chelpark rains

ink fight evidence, amoeboid stains

dodging the conductor

asking for your tickets

playing with a stolen ball

one bounce cricket

yes, they all hide in there

in that little box, that's where

these are but a few

of the 100's inside

hidden away for a rainy day

a day of dark and gloom

to brighten up my sagging mood

perhaps, do me some good

but, every time i try

to find that little box

the one with Tiger locks

it seems to run

to hide away

it seems to hate the sun

so, i wait for that

that lucky day,

when the box will, again

come my way

it has a will, all its own

like me, it wishes to be alone.

12841 Superfast

it cuts

through the stormy night

grumbling

a seething metal millipede

with luminous eyes

its feet clatter

as they turn around

a rhythm to inspire

music

or a pyre

in its body

it jealously holds

the 1000 lives

it bought

with tickets sold

little paper stubs

printed 'berth' control

it screams at night

a banshee shriek

it protests a red light

its got a schedule to keep

muck escapes its underbelly

human debris

staining beams of Burma teak

beneath

it has no regard

no remorse

no feeling

stepping in its path

the grim reapers calling

in its belly

sit wannabe brides

dowry negotiators

rapists, dacoits

it's the symbol of a nation

united by hate

get a student concession

for a slimy politician

or an out-of-turn seat

you don't need permission

you can buy anger

from a tea vendor

a signal falls

out of turn

sleep-laden eyelids

flutter in vain

a line change effected

a phone call rejected

a quarter bottle

lies empty

a beedi extinguished

it screams

once again

but this time

it's different

harmonies of pain

fear sings the seconds

it falters

it rocks

its arrogance shattered

it's shocked

surprised

this wasn't supposed to happen

296 lives

lie gripped

in mangled arms of steel

scarlet lines connect

as they bleed

castes religion and creed

just a stutter

on the PA

a hesitant blip

the announcement continues

'the next train will leave

from platform number 2'.

I wished...

i wished

upon a shooting star

it fell

down in ashes

i wished

on 2 ravens

but one

flew away

i wished

with a coin

in a well

it was dry

i wished

on a candle

on the icing

it died

i wished

on a dandelion

but whiskers

it had none

i wished

on an eyelash

but it stuck

to my hand

i wished

on a tree

they cut it

for a pyre

i wished

on a new moon

not knowing

of its eclipse

i wished

on a bone

but it poked

my hand

i wished

you'd read

this poem

but you

skipped the page.

Night

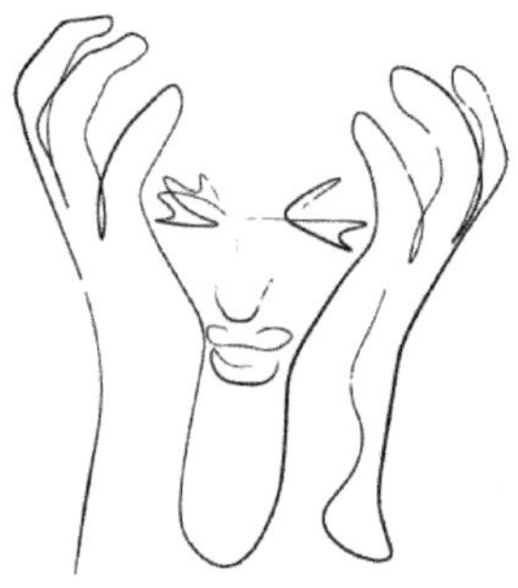

agony creeps, a bandicoot at night

carrying anguish, an aching soul fights

distress echoes, hollow, empty pain

suffering's dark shadow remains.

torment's fiery flames, deep red inside

affliction's weight brushes hope aside

grief, like a knife, serrated, piercing

wounds, scars and hearts bleeding

nagging voices of disregard don't cease

the dull throbbing ache, brings no release

dark waves, crash on sorrow's shore

with a bitter spray, regrets galore

the hollow ache of longing won't mend

dark veils of misery, sorrow portend

relentless pain, grips, holds tight

painful reminder of an endless night.

Write Reason

Why do i write?

sometimes

i wonder.

express my views

opinions too

define my prejudice

in words unsubtle

my bias vacillates

ideology unsettled

Why do i write?

sometimes

i ponder.

exposing my pain

my deepest fears too

calling out deceit

hypocrisy and hate

showcasing shame

with impotent rage

Why do i write?

sometimes

i wonder.

externalise feelings

therapeutic they said

put it all out

bloodletting does good

when there's nothing to hide

there's nothing to fight

Why do i write?

sometimes

i ponder.

somebody out there

should know you're alive

stir the hornet's hive

throw a pebble

start a ripple

in the still pond of life

Why do i write?

sometimes

i wonder.

now it's all done

i've scribbled it out

every conviction every doubt

a verbal striptease

i'm naked. i'm jaded.

unashamedly exposed

Why do i write?

sometimes

i ponder.

will you judge me now

draw your own conclusion

paint me in the colours

of muddled consternation

will you think of me now

differently somehow

Why do i write?

sometimes

i wonder.

I Do.

One for the road

he stepped out

his thoughts

afire

his fingers trembled

unsatiated

desire

his focus was singular

escape

go under

he hated

what he loved

he abhorred

the need

abject servitude

but she held him

in her arms

unyielding

her smell

enchanting

his tears

had dried

his anger

raged free

no justification

no explanation

detoxification

isolation

his vision

had cleared

only to deceive

she beckoned

he fell

leaving everything

incomplete

respect

love

shame

and honour

he couldn't move

beyond her

her toxic embrace

he fought

but he didn't

he resisted

but he couldn't

she stalked him

not letting go

print

press

television

radio

there's no getting away

he knew it

now

the calling too strong

the bond

a love

gone wrong

she wasn't far now

across the road

her home

shimmered

an alcoholic mirage

an oasis

her heaven

he stumbled

vacant eyed

wobbly limbed

he didn't hear

the 'thunk'

of flesh against metal

he didn't see

the crowd

didn't hear

the screams

he didn't see

the drunk

across the street

unseeing

the drunk shuffled

to her dirty abode

drank off her breasts

'one for the road'.

Different

i've never

thought it strange

though others

think it's weird

i have a different view

some say it's absurd

the ocean is secretive

i think

why else would she speak

with waves that say sssshh?

the trees have Parkinson's

their leaves tremble

fear is wintry

of that i am sure

chills down your spine

then a long shiver

paddy fields are oceans

in green disguise

dams are cholesterol blocks

release valves and locks

volcanoes like pimples erupt

pain and scars

destruction and hurt

flowers are messengers

of elusive joy

very few are perennial

they bloom they die

deserts are but sandy slates

for winds to sketch upon

when tired of the heat

there's always the pond

finger trails on sand or water

the wind doesn't care

it doesn't matter

the clouds, earth's thoughts

cumulus, nimbus, stratus

always moving about

which brings me

to mine

as i sit on the cliff

life is behind me

the outlook divine

i breathe in the air

the layered perfume

i smile.

i'm different.

time to jump

time to fly.

Lost and found

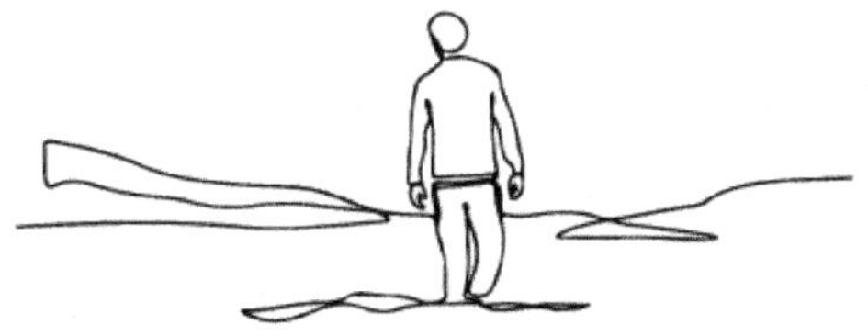

in the depths of memory,

a treasure trove lies

where lost moments

thoughts

and dreams arise

every splinter every shard

every piece

now is found

and brought to release

the knotted threads

of a tapestry so fine

rewoven now

to a picture divine

past whispers

once faint and cold

echo loud

stories to be told

in the auricles of the heart

where love resides

every tear

every sorrow abides

splinters of shattered hopes

now made whole

reflecting the beauty

of a tired soul

every step every fall

every stumble and strife

led to this moment

where all is right

in the journey

i have found

all that is lost

despite sacrifices made

at a heavy cost

all that was lost

has been found

it's true

it's time to wake up

begin anew

Horrorscope

time to get hooked

time to get married

your biological clock is ticking

you're getting old

i was told

check on the stars

the planets too

their positions

matter

affect you.

rahu in the 4th house

ketu is not

mercury is ascending

honestly

so what?

he's from a good family

post graduate too

talk to him

they said

why don't you?

i'm into s and m

some bondage too

surely that's no problem

you'll enjoy it too

he said.

this boy is a find

no bad habits

such a mama's boy

guess i'll be

his favourite toy.

no working after marriage

no protest no choice

spread your legs

bear me 3 boys.

what do you mean

ambition

what bloody career

cover your head

with your pallu

wherever you appear.

he said

don't check me out

my insta account

my bumble page

my girlfriend count

i'm a man

you're not

let there be no doubt.

go on

toe the line.

behave.

sure, your daddy paid

but you are mine

i smiled

i smirked.

reached into my purse

pulled out a smoke.

drank from my hip flask

a Glenlivet neat

eyes popped out.

the fat lady screamed.

B.A; B.Ed.

he'd sit in the corner

half in the dark

eyes hunting

betel-stained dhoti

a khadi cloth top

burnt sienna teeth

art he would teach

to pig-tailed little girls

budding breasts

eyes wide in wonder

brush strokes not adept

looking up to their teacher

i'll hold your hand

let me help you

he'd say

one hand brushing

the other one stroking

sorry ma

don't mind

it's nothing

he'd say

she'd smile

unsure

he seemed so benign

nobody taught her

bad touch from good

but something was wrong

feel it she could

sit on my lap

don't mind the bump

he'd say

just push it to the side

it'll make it go away

hold it now

gently

stroke it up and down

into a lecherous grin

his face would transform

hands would pretend

to tighten a bow

that was lovely

he'd say

you can go

ask your friend to come

i'll teach her too

but keep it a secret

between me and you

his little betel box

would open with a click

blood red relief

betel stains betrayed belief

checked shirts

tainted lives

innocence shattered

watercolours splattered

between the prussian blue

and the post office red

lay the lives of children

on which he'd tread

she remembers him well

as she flips through her yearbook

his legacy is painted

on the walls of her school

a great art teacher

so good with the children

he's touched their lives

little Monets and Reuben

between the crayons and pastels

the watercolour and oils

hung the portraits of lives

completely destroyed

he's gone now

at last

finally put to rest

but the memories of him

she still does dread

suresh mama

B.A; B.Ed.

Ants

These are my thoughts

Little squiggles

On paper

Black

Little ants

All in a row

Scurrying about

Looking busy as hell

Sometimes all organised

Sometimes pell-mell

Just searching

Expressing

Exploring

Exposing

Little black ants

Never resting

Never tiring

Never sleeping

Never stopping.

What if?

haven't you wondered

often

what if?

what if

you'd taken

the road more travelled

what if

you'd eloped

not got married

what if

you'd called

tails not head

what if

you'd chosen

art not med

what if

you'd taken

the train you missed

what if

you'd been sober

not totally pissed

what if

you'd voted

and not abstained

what if

your words

were never restrained

what if

you'd apologised

not remained stubborn

what if

you'd been caught

watching internet porn

what if

you'd never

to an ideology align

what if

life wasn't

about 6's and 9's

what if

you'd listened

to that fortune teller

what if

the parrot

could've made your life better

what if

you'd got 6

when you rolled the dice

what if

you'd refused

to listen to advise

what if

you'd chosen

horoscopes over love

what if

you'd given up

when push came to shove

what if

you'd accepted

you didn't know it all

what if

it never made

a difference at all

what if

life wasn't

preordained by the gods

what if

your choices

were all that you got

what if

you could do it

all over again

what if

you weren't sure

it would bring any change

what if

the toast

never had butter

what if

grass here

was always better

what if

there were never

2 birds in the bush

what if

in the race

the rats were in no rush

what if

all was real

nothing an illusion

what if

you lived

in constant delusion

what if

every beginning

didn't need an end

what if

every black cat

didn't misfortune portend

what if

Newton was wrong

his 3rd law a fake

what if

you were to blame

for all your mistakes

what if

time stood still

would you continue to move

what if

there was

nothing to prove

what if

you'd never

picked up this book

what if

what if

if not

what if?

Obituary

i slept

for years

a social slumber

far from people

and their inquisitive ears

forgotten time

pickled

in a jar

memories

like moss grew

spores and mildew

wake up

i did

with a habit morbid

i loved reading

obituaries

i truly did

anthony das

at the lord's feet

yagnaraman

found eternal peace

gunathilaka

may you find nirvana

she's in the arms of god

josephine hannah

some friends

some strangers

acquaintances too

some fading pictures

in an old yearbook

some paper cuttings

from a drama review

some smiling in death

in black and white

some looking morose

no resurrection in sight

yes

i read them

it's an absolute must

ashes to ashes

dust to dust

this morning's column

is different though

not many have died

it seems so

just one dead face

stares blankly at me

vacant eyes boast

of some random degree

i look once more

he's strangely familiar

a face from the mirror

not just a stranger

i smile

it's a sign

the obituary

it's mine.

Uncertain Verse

when i sit here musing

it is often confusing

the words just flow

from thought to text

sometimes they rhyme

sometimes they don't

what's with these sentences?

one

word

lines

sometimes two

some have a tune

some tumble out too soon

some need a rethink

isn't quite what i inked

some need an edit

some are intricately linked

i try to explore

meter

and style

my thoughts forsake me

lost in poetic prosody

spondee

anapest

pyrrhic

trochee

i don't understand

what they're meant to be

is this how i think

in stutters and spurts

improbable association

verbal exploration

is this the way forward

from random

thought

to text

from heartbeat

to breath

should one sit and reflect

put words in context

adjust the phrasing

to fit into a metre

modify expression

into pentameter

the idea seems twisted

maybe it's time tested

maybe it's a rule

meant for some other fool

i couldn't care less

this is my universe

25 completed

in Uncertain Verse.